CLEETHORPES COMES TO PARIS

Malcolm Carson

All rights reserved. No part of this work covered by the copyright hereon may be reproduced or used in any means – graphic, electronic, or mechanical, including copying, recording, taping, or information storage and retrieval systems – without written permission of the publisher.

Printed by Russell Press Limited
Russell House, Bulwell Lane, Basford, Nottingham NG6 0BT
(0115) 978 4505

Typeset by narrator
www.narrator.me.uk
info@narrator.me.uk

Published by Shoestring Press
19 Devonshire Avenue, Beeston, Nottingham, NG9 1BS
(0115) 925 1827
www.shoestringpress.co.uk

First published 2014
© Copyright: Malcolm Carson

The moral right of the author has been asserted.

ISBN 978 1 907356 60 5

ACKNOWLEDGEMENTS

Thanks are due to the editors of the following in which some of the poems first appeared:

Great River Review, Anderson Center for Interdisciplinary Studies, Minnesota, USA.

The Dock website: http://www.thedock.info

Thanks also to Abegail Morley for her early advice with some of the poems.

TOUT DROIT

Calais. Abroad. 'Pardon, monsieur,
quelle est la route à Paris?'
It was as if the bits of a puzzle
begun at school should make sense.
Was this what I'd endured
Ces Smith for, his aertex Y-fronts
pulled over shirt tails,
the caresses then slaps
of the Gaffer, whom we detested?
Would this old geezer know our French?
'Tout droit, tout droit!' he said.
Tout is *all*, *droit* is *right*,
so keep going right, we surmised.
Sometime later, and no lifts,
we returned to the familiar spot,
contempt for my teachers
confirmed, for what did they know
about France, real French?

AUTOSTOP

We'd wonder who we'd get,
as no doubt did they
in their approach,
a moment to suss us out,
pull in. Destination settled
we'd start a conversation
as though to pay them back,
each phrase assessed, developed
or let drop if conflict was foreseen.
It was as if we'd entered
their favourite sitting room
or just as intimate
at any rate, where taste
and manners, predilections
and prejudice were on
display as they might parade
their new-bought suite. Or else
we'd learn of problems
only strangers learn,
their secrets safe in our rucksacks.
Sometimes resentment stirred,
their chances lost to do
the same as us. Others though
were content with silence,
the hum of company enough
until we'd disembark
and leave their lives, our brief
acquaintance vapourised
down the fast receding road.

BOIS DE BOULOGNE

Paris. For now a park of camper vans, tents,
and Al and I with bed rolls from Millets.
Night arrival. We took possession of
our allocated pitch, too grand by half,
laid out our beds with such authority
as we could muster, unrolled our new identities,
sure we would find what we had read about
in books, the record sleeves, had tasted
in Gauloises, rehearsed in imagined lives,
real loves. And now, to be part of this...
Damp morning, we wiped the slug trails off our bags,
beating the bourgeois rush to toilet blocks,
descended into the Métro of our hopes.

LIVRE DE POCHE

We met around the record shop,
drawn by jazz as if on cue,
Karl-Heinz, Rob Stalk and others,
from exotic places then: Cologne,
Amsterdam, and Cleethorpes.
With jazz we held our own:
the endless hours of favourite tracks,
the lists of personnel, the greats we'd heard.
Yet it was the *Librairies*
that drew us most and those little books
economy-sized, functional,
their yen for subversion.
We'd ration our hours along the shelves,
the carousels, swap authors
we knew or ought to know,
ignore the glossier pretenders
not worthy of our shared confidence,
our new confederacy.

CHEZ POPOFF

Une nouvelle vague de beatniks
was how we read of ourselves,
squatting on the pavement,
backs to Popoff's, rue de la Huchette.
This was all I could have dreamed of,
had read about. Taken in
by this Russian émigré, we sat around
spending as little as we could,
stored much in memories,
talked of Sartre, poetry, jazz:
too easy to parody now.
Hughes and Gunn in my pocket,
I felt parochial. So did Al;
I caught him at the Gare du Nord,
boarding the train for Cleethorpes.

MEMPHIS SLIM

Straight back, you're fine, I called
as he shunted his restless Jag
in that kennel of a street outside
the club. He opened the door
of his smile: *Why, thank you!*
Better than any autograph, that.
Huge and glistening, he hunched
down the steps to sing the blues,
and I, a doctor's son,
banked my privilege.

SHAKESPEARE ET CIE

You're quite a bibliophile, aren't you?
His cultured New England voice
roused me from the books,
the taking of tea and Jacques Loussier.
Here I was in breathing distance
of Hemingway, Joyce, Sylvia Beach,
Beckett – Shakespeare and company.
And then addressed by the dispenser
of tea and reputations! So far
from lunchtimes in that Lincolnshire
market town and snatched moments
of Larkin, Hughes, Chekhov…
Like grubbing taties in the muck-hill.

A few weeks on, the dust of Spain
and *autostop* silting my clothes,
I was not welcome, transformed for him
into a rootless vagabond.
His anger drove me out.
Straightway I was back in Louth,
the auctioneer's pupil, anxious,
groping after something else.
But then I shook from my feet
the dust of that august shop,
and write about it now.

CLOCHARD

'Round midnight when we saw her
haunched to piss, the pavement
flowed until she upped her drawers

alert now to our approach. *Clochard,*
we said, held back, watching
her embarrassed shadow skulk

against the Sorbonne's gothic walls.
We were for a time a part of this –
soup kitchen queues (shut down

when fights broke out), the 'conning'
for a franc, baguette or chocolate,
looking for a place to kip

in derelict, *chantier* or open van.
More often than not we'd end up
half-asleep in Popoff's mid-afternoon

or moved on from Seine's warm banks.
Such joy there was despite discomfort,
the living out our existential dream
with foreign girls, much cooler than ourselves.

PARIS BRÛLE-T-IL?

Sloughing off our sleeping bags,
builder's sand in hair and eyes,
we pushed aside the boards
and blinked into another time
where swastikas hung
over Liberté, Fraternité,
Egalité, and marching columns
passed across the square,
stamping time aside.
Karl-Heinz and I stood aghast
– 'Un vrai cauchemar' –
until we saw the cameras, directors
and sundry crew in a time we knew
as ours. Despite relief the look
between us spoke of how we might
have been assigned our differing roles
had we not had our generation's luck.

PÈRE-LACHAISE

Beside pollarded alder
a metal crown of thorns
embraces the child
weeping to heaven.
Beneath, destinations
of transportees to Sachsenhausen,
Ravensbruck, Buchenwald.
Easy to hear in those names
thuggishness, brutality,
a guttural boot.
Yet Sachsenhausen,
much later, I was told,
'is such a pretty place'.
How pretty too 'Milice',
light and French.
Enamelled photographs,
the blazing geranium
on raked gravel,
testaments in kitsch
in a sanctuary of sorts.
We maunder among
the gothic graves
which elevate the bourgeoisie
with porticos, pilasters,
a sculpted palm, toward
perimeter wall,
engraved by bullets
where last Communards
were slaughtered.
Tourists, maps flapping
seek out Piaf, Wilde
as cats caterwaul,
spray their patch.

THE KIP

By the candle of his lighter
he plumped up the vein
on ankle's taut map.
Shadows morphed
against roof beams,
needle seeming to buckle
as though under water.
A scuffle of voices,
conspiracy of silence,
a change of state.
Here in the attic, derelict,
I grew into my bag
quiet, discreet, smelt
myself for comfort,
now knew the border
of my dreams.